MOVIEMAKERS' FILM CLUB

Be a
SCREENWRITER

Turn Your Idea into a SCRIPT

PowerKiDS press

Alix Wood

New York

Published in 2018 by Rosen Publishing
29 East 21st Street, New York, NY 10010

CATALOGING-IN-PUBLICATION DATA
Names: Wood, Alix.
Title: Be a screenwriter: turn your idea into a script / Alix Wood.
Description: New York : PowerKids Press, 2018. | Series: Moviemakers' film club |
    Includes index.
Identifiers: LCCN ISBN 9781538323786 (pbk.) | ISBN 9781538322802 (library bound) |
    ISBN 9781538323793 (6 pack)
Subjects: LCSH: Motion picture authorship--Juvenile literature.
Classification: LCC PN1996.W64 2018 | DDC 808.2'3--dc23

Produced for Rosen Publishing by Alix Wood Books
Designed by Alix Wood
Editor: Eloise Macgregor
Editor for Rosen: Kerri O'Donnell
Series consultant: Cameron Browne

Photo credits: Cover, 1, 5, 6, 7, 8, 12, 13, 15, 16, 18, 20, 21, 22, 23, 25, 26-27, 28 top
© Adobe Stock Images; 4 Shutterstock/PR Image Factory; 9 Shutterstock/India Picture;
13 Shutterstock/Cookie Studio.10, 17 © Alix Wood; 28 bottom © Cameron Browne

Printed in the United States of America

CPSIA compliance information: Batch #BW18PK: For further information contact
Rosen Publishing, New York, New York at 1-800-542-2595.

CONTENTS

Introducing the Screenwriter! 4

Starting from a Book 6

Thinking Up a Story 8

The Nitty Gritty 10

Characters 12

Deciding on a Setting 14

Writing in Scenes 16

Cutting from One Scene to Another 18

Writing Dialogue 20

Giving Directions 22

The Final Tweaks 24

Getting Your Screenplay Noticed 26

Action! 28

Glossary 30

For More Information 31

Index 32

INTRODUCING THE SCREENWRITER!

You walk into the movie studio, check in at reception, and wait, nervously. You get taken up to the meeting room. The decision-makers are sitting around the table, waiting for you. You have planned the whole movie in your head. Now is the moment of truth. If the studio likes your idea, you get the job. If they don't, that is months of work wasted.

Screenwriters write **scripts** for movies. It is a very creative job. They must turn a blank page into a living, breathing world full of characters with a story to tell. The script is the starting point for most movies. Screenwriters create the **dialogue**, characters, and story line.

A screenwriter needs to ...

- be able to write well
- have creativity and imagination
- have good storytelling skills
- understand how a story is structured
- be able to accept criticism
- be able to cope with their work being rejected
- have good presentation and **networking** skills
- love writing scripts!

Cell Phone Movie School

Screenwriters often base their characters on real people they come across. They may overhear a conversation on a train that sparks the idea for a character. Listening to how different people speak will help you write using someone else's voice. If you want to become a screenwriter, start watching and listening to the world around you.

"To make a great film you need three things - the script, the script, and the script."

Alfred Hitchcock

Screenwriters might specialize in writing one type of movie, such as comedy, drama, or science fiction.

STARTING FROM A BOOK

So how do you start writing your screenplay? A blank page can be scary. It might be easier to work with the characters and **plot** from something already written. Screenwriters often adapt books into screenplays. Can you think of a story that you love that might make a good movie?

When an author writes a book, they can write what the characters are thinking. You can't describe in words what someone is thinking in a screenplay. A screenwriter can still help show a character's emotions through their writing, though. They can show how a character reacts to a situation. A child might see some bullies coming toward them. Do they run or stand up to them? Their reaction says a lot about what the character is feeling, and about their personality.

Using Symbols

A screenwriter can also use **symbolism** to show emotion. Perhaps someone whose child is missing could be shown hugging their teddy bear. A screenwriter can give brief directions to an actor on how to play a character, too.

Make the Story into Something New

It may not work to copy the original story exactly. Just taking dialogue straight from a book and putting it in your script doesn't always work well. You may want your dialogue to tell more of the story that you can't directly tell your audience.

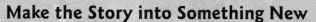

Choosing Your Book

All kinds of books would make a good movie. Usually, when you read a book, you imagine what the characters and setting look like. When you choose your story, pick one that you can clearly imagine. You'll find it easier to **visualize** your movie because you can already "see" it.

Choose a story that you can film easily. This movie would need a pirate ship and special effects! Will your budget stretch that far?

THINKING UP A STORY

You may already have a story in your head that you think would make a great movie. If so, you are on your way to creating a great screenplay. Don't worry if you haven't got an idea yet though. Try some of these tips to get you started.

- Think of your favorite movie. Were there any things you would change about it? What? Focus on that change. Could you create a whole story around your new idea?

- Read the news. The news has a daily stream of great plot ideas. Make sure you change the names and the details a little, to make it your own story.

- Listen to song lyrics, watch TV, and read. All of these can spark an idea for a screenplay.

- Keep a diary. Your own experiences may make a great story.

"'Write every day, line by line, page by page, hour by hour."

Robert McKee

Try to think about your audience. They might inspire you. Are you writing this for adults, kids, or families? Do you want to make people laugh, gasp, or even cry? Maybe your mom loves a good chase scene, or your brother likes animal movies. Write with an audience in mind.

Planning Your Story

Once you have your idea, it is time to work on your plot. The plot is the main story line of your movie and usually roughly follows the stages below:

- Introduce your hero
- Put them in a new situation
- Give your hero a goal
- Follow their progress toward their goal
- Add a complication
- Your hero must risk everything to succeed
- The big ending
- Your hero's new life

Cell Phone Movie School

Suffering from **writer's block**? Writer's block is when you come across an obstacle and just can't seem to move your story forward. Don't stare at a blank page for too long. Instead, work on a different part of the story. That may help your writing to start flowing again, and you are more likely to think up a solution.

THE NITTY GRITTY

Screenplays are written in a special **format**. They don't look anything like a book. If you want to hit the big time, write your screenplay in the right format. It will make you look very professional! Some free software programs, such as Celtx, will help format a script for you. Big Hollywood producers simply won't read a script if it is not presented in the right way.

Make a title page for the front cover of your script.

A title page shows the screenplay's title, author's name, and contact details. Type the title in bold in the center of the page. Then type "Written by" and your name centered underneath the title. At the bottom right-hand corner type your name and contact details.

THE FIRE MONSTER

Written by
Sammy Hampshire

Sammy Hampshire,
465 North Street, Saunderstone,
AZ 85000
Tel: 0123 4567891

Professional script readers say they can usually tell if a screenplay is going to be good after reading a few pages. They prefer an easy-to-read script full of action with no long, boring, descriptive paragraphs.

FADE IN:

EXT. A CABIN IN WOODS - DUSK

A bear rustles through a trash can.

TOM and RUTH appear walking through the trees. The bear runs off.

> TOM
> Did you hear that?

> RUTH
> (startled)
> What was it?

TOM shrugs his shoulders

> RUTH (CONT'D)
> Let's get inside, quick.

Where the action takes place. EXT. means exterior, INT. means interior.

Place page numbers at the top right corner

Put character names in capital letters. Character cues are 4.2 inches (10.7 cm) from left margin or centered.

Place stage directions 3.6 inches (9.1 cm) from the left margin.

Keep dialogue 2.9 inches (7.4 cm) from the left margin.

Leave a 1-inch (2.5 cm) margin top, right, and bottom, and 1.5 inches (3.8 cm) on the left for hole-punching.

Cell Phone Movie School

Feature film scripts are usually 90 – 120 pages long. Around 100 – 110 pages is ideal. Movie studios and theater owners prefer movies that last two hours or less, so theaters can show them as many times a day as possible. To help judge how long a script will take to film, screenwriters type their scripts using a **typeface** named Courier, at a certain size, 12 **point**. This typeface roughly averages one minute of film time per page.

Courier 12pt

CHARACTERS

When you think of a favorite movie, you probably remember the hero or heroes of the story. The best way to draw in an audience is to give them unforgettable characters. Some screenwriters write their main character first. They then think up a plot to suit them, rather than make the character suit the plot. So how do you start to think up your great characters?

- Use real people as a basis for your character. Think of people you like or don't like at all. Use their qualities to shape your character's personality.

- Give your character a face. This can help you picture the character better in your head. You can imagine the face of someone you know, or use a famous person's appearance to give to your character.

You can use **archetypes** in your screenwriting, too. An archetype is a very typical example of a certain person. Perhaps your character could be a wise, old man, or an evil villain. Make your archetype unique by mixing in new characteristics. Maybe your wise, old man could be a liar, or very forgetful?

Get to know your characters. What do they do when they're
not facing adventure in your screenplay? Do they have hobbies?
What's their favorite meal? Knowing your characters well helps
you make them more convincing in your story.

A name might inspire a character.
Have a look through a baby name
book. Pick a name and then choose
a surname. Try to imagine what
your new character would be like.

Adding in some habits or
mannerisms can make your
character very believable.
Maybe they take off their
glasses when they're thinking,
or drum on the table with
their fingers.

DECIDING ON A SETTING

The "when" and the "where" can be as important as the "who" and the "what" in a screenplay. Setting the scene for your movie can have a big influence on the feel of it. Do you want your movie set in modern times, or in the past? Is it set in outer space, or a city, or the desert? There are so many choices. You need to decide what will best suit your characters and your plot.

Getting to Know Your Setting

The setting should be like another character. As the scriptwriter, you need to get to know your setting and be able to picture it in your head. If you are setting your movie in the past or future, do some research to get all the little details right. Don't have a character in the 1960s using a cell phone!

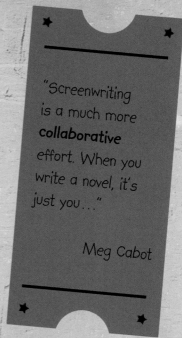

"Screenwriting is a much more **collaborative** effort. When you write a novel, it's just you ..."

Meg Cabot

A well-written screenplay needs to say just enough to tell the reader where the story is set, and give a general feel of the place. It is important to leave the detail up to the director or set designer. They will want to make those decisions.

```
INT. A MODERN, BARE, UPSTAIRS
OFFICE, JUST DESK, CHAIR, AND PHONE
- DAY

TOM is slumped in the chair staring
out of the large picture window,
looking bored.
```

Writing for the Camera

The first shot of a new **scene** that shows where the action is taking place is known as an **establishing shot**. It usually shows the exterior of the building, or the neighborhood. When you write a description of the setting, picture the establishing shot in your head.

Using Dialogue

Another way to establish the setting is to have your characters actually talk about it. You will quickly know the action is set on a dairy farm if your characters are talking about getting up in time for milking.

Adding Subtitles

Subtitles can help show the time and place. Your establishing shot may show a desert landscape, but which desert, where? You can add a subtitle like: "SONOMA DESERT – JULY,1985."

Cell Phone Movie School

When you choose your setting, make sure it is somewhere you can easily recreate when you come to film your movie. If you live in a city, it may be tricky if you set your story in the desert.

WRITING IN SCENES

Now that you have decided on your plot, characters, and setting, you need to give your story a structure. Most movies consist of three main **acts**. The first act sets up the story. The second act introduces an obstacle. The third act confronts the obstacle and leads to a **resolution**. Within your screenplay's acts are smaller sections of action known as scenes.

A scene is a part of the movie that is set in a particular time and place. At the beginning of each scene, you should state whether it's interior or exterior, where the scene is taking place, and what time of day it is.

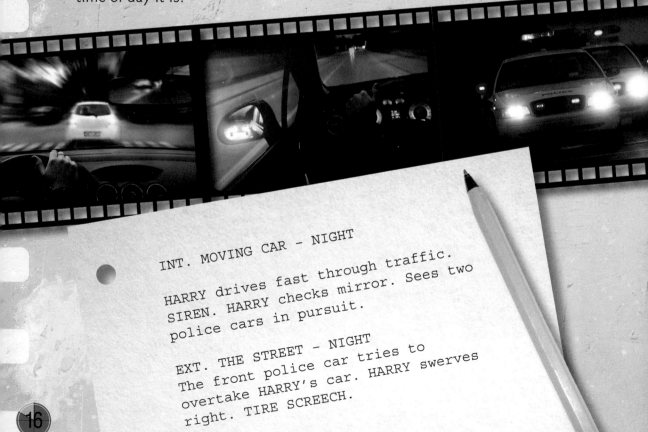

```
INT. MOVING CAR - NIGHT
HARRY drives fast through traffic.
SIREN. HARRY checks mirror. Sees two
police cars in pursuit.

EXT. THE STREET - NIGHT
The front police car tries to
overtake HARRY's car. HARRY swerves
right. TIRE SCREECH.
```

Your first act is very important. It introduces the characters and story. The first few pages of your script have to grab your audience's attention. If your Hollywood script reader is bored by the end of the first few pages, they will put down your script and reach for the next one.

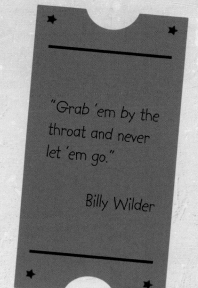

"Grab 'em by the throat and never let 'em go."

Billy Wilder

It is important that each scene has a point, and that something happens in it that is important to the whole movie.

Cell Phone Movie School

If a scene doesn't work, you can be sure the director or the editor will **cut** it. Try these tips to make sure each scene you write is the best it can be.

- As you write each scene, ask yourself what needs to happen in it to move the plot forward.

- Shut your eyes and try to picture your scene as though it was already filmed. That process will help show you if your scene works or not.

- Don't set every scene somewhere obvious. Maybe your characters could argue waiting at the veterinarian's office with their cat, instead of around the kitchen table at home.

CUTTING FROM ONE SCENE TO ANOTHER

Scriptwriters need to have a way of making it obvious to their audience that one scene has ended and another has begun. Changing from one scene to another is called a **transition**. Mainly, transitions are decided by film editors, after the film has been shot. An editor might decide to cut or to gradually fade into the next scene, for instance.

Scriptwriters may need to write in a particular transition if it is essential to the story. For instance, you might use a **dissolve shot** to show some time has passed. A dissolve shot shows one shot dissolving away as the next shot appears underneath it at the same time. The images briefly overlap.

A scriptwriter might want a dissolve shot to show this boy remembering his siblings. A simple cut to them playing would not have shown that so well.

Transitions Screenwriters Might Use

- Music or sound playing over the end of one scene to the next scene.

- A cut known as a **misdirect** makes the audience believe a shot is still part of the first scene, but is gradually revealed to be a new scene. For example, a close-up of a car tire rolling along a road in one scene could pull back to show it is now a motorcycle tire on a dirt track in a new scene.

- Ending a scene with a question, and then showing the possible answer to that question at the start of the next scene.

- Linking an image at the end of a scene with an image at the start of the next, such as blowing out a candle before a cut to a sunset.

- Going from a **close shot** to a **wide shot**, but only put an instruction like this in your script if it helps explain something in the story.

"Transitions are a super important part of moving from one scene to the next..."

Craig Mazin

Cell Phone Movie School

Busy script readers get bored by too many instructions and skip over them. Only use transitions in your script when they are necessary to move the story along. Save your big transitions for key moments in your screenplay, when you really need the reader to notice them.

WRITING DIALOGUE

In a screenplay, the dialogue is really important. It has to be interesting, help drive the plot forward, and sound realistic. At the same time, you mustn't bore your audience. People's day-to-day speech can be dull, or full of "umms" and "uhhs." Screen dialogue needs to be like we speak, but more interesting!

Get Real

Use **abbreviations**, so your dialogue sounds more natural. Say "Don't shoot!" rather than "Do not shoot!" Read every line out loud. Think about the situation the character is in, and decide if each line is right for that character at that time. Ask a friend to read your script and see if they think the dialogue sounds real.

Keeping It Tight

Ask yourself if your dialogue is necessary. If it isn't, cut it. Long, boring conversations will make a dull scene. Your audience may tune out. Keep everything your characters say short and punchy.

Don't say:

"I think there may be a problem with the rotor blade. It might be a good idea for everyone to get off the helicopter immediately."

Do say:

"Get off this helicopter, NOW!"

Cell Phone Movie School

Try to make each character speak with their own unique voice. They may have favorite words they use, or ways of saying things. If you could cover up a character's name and still know who was talking, then your dialogue is perfect!

Rookie Mistakes

- *Writing pages of dialogue with no action.* Movies are visual, so we need to see things happening. It doesn't have to be a car chase, just something we can see.

- *Characters telling us what we are already seeing.* If you have told us we can see Harry jumping from a building, there's no need to have a character say "Harry's jumping from the building."

You can get a character to **voice-over** action. Write "V.O." next to the speaker.

HARRY (V.O.)
Lucky I liked parkour as a kid!

GIVING DIRECTIONS

In a movie, actions speak louder than words. While dialogue is important, directions give your screenplay its action. You may want to show how something should be said, or let the reader know that an action should take place. You do this by writing brief directions.

Actor's Directions

Some directions are called **parentheticals** because you place them between parentheses. You can show emotion in parentheses.

If you want to show an important pause in your dialogue, you use the word "beat" in parentheses.

```
INT. INTERVIEW ROOM - NIGHT

          VICTOR
     (choking back tears)
I've never seen that gun
before. Honestly, I,...
(beat) it's really not
my gun.
```

Actors don't like being told how to act any more than directors like being told how to direct! Only use directions if they are really necessary.

Some stage directions help anyone reading your script be aware of what we can see in a scene, for example "INT. INTERVIEW ROOM - NIGHT (GUN in evidence bag on desk)" This information is important to the story. Directions are also used to describe anything we hear that's not dialogue. It is not necessary to describe the scenery in detail.

How to Write Good Directions

- First, think "Do I really need to write this direction at all?"
- Keep the direction short
- Don't use fancy language
- Don't do other people's jobs, such as describing the set in detail. That's the set designer's decision
- Write in the present tense – "JOHN picks up a knife," not "picked"

Cell Phone Movie School

What if you really want a **close-up** shot but don't want to insult the director by saying so? Try being subtle. Put in a direction such as "JOHN's eyes widen". To show this, the director really has no choice but to do a close-up!

THE FINAL TWEAKS

How do you know when your script is finished? You should keep rewriting until you can't improve your story any more. Here are some simple things to check to see if your script has had all its final tweaks.

Read it through out loud to yourself. It's a great way to pick up any parts that are too dull. Even better, get a few friends together and read through out loud. Then your friends can give you their views on whether any parts don't really work well. Sometimes it is hard to listen to criticism from other people, but if it helps get a better finished screenplay, it's worth it!

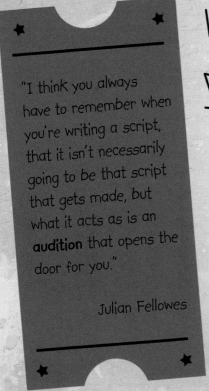

"I think you always have to remember when you're writing a script, that it isn't necessarily going to be that script that gets made, but what it acts as is an **audition** that opens the door for you."

Julian Fellowes

Cell Phone Movie School

Want a good way to check that each character's voice keeps consistent? Go through the whole script just reading one character at a time. Ask yourself if their dialogue stays in character. Do they always use a certain way to greet people? Do they have favorite phrases? A voice may change for a reason — for example, the character might grow in confidence during the story.

Cut It Out

Read through your least favorite scene. Are there ways that you can improve it? What is it you don't like? Maybe change the setting, or the weather? Or, if it doesn't move your plot forward, why not cut the scene out entirely?

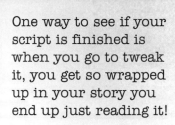

One way to see if your script is finished is when you go to tweak it, you get so wrapped up in your story you end up just reading it!

Pick a Great Title

You may already have your movie title in mind when you write your script. If not, this is one very important final tweak. It will be the first thing a movie studio reads when they pick up your script. Does it sell your idea, and get readers wanting to know more? Most of the best movie titles are short and catchy, usually three words or less. Most titles are either the main character's name (*Shrek*), a place or thing (*Labyrinth*), or an event (*Star Wars*).

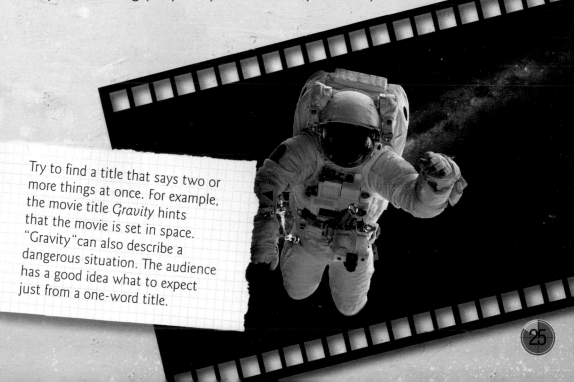

Try to find a title that says two or more things at once. For example, the movie title *Gravity* hints that the movie is set in space. "Gravity" can also describe a dangerous situation. The audience has a good idea what to expect just from a one-word title.

GETTING YOUR SCREENPLAY NOTICED

Scriptwriting can be a lonely job. Unlike other roles in the movie industry, you may be sitting alone in a room working away day and night. So, once you have written your blockbuster, you need to get it out there. How?

- You may have a group of friends who want to make a movie. Working together would be a great way to help make your screenplay come to life.

- You could send your script to a screenwriting competition. Most competitions ask for some money to pay for the time someone has to spend reading through your script, though. Try looking for competitions that are free to send your script to.

- Scriptwriting festivals will often help young writers with their scripts by holding workshops and lectures. See if there are any festivals in your area that you could attend.

- Look for movie production companies that might read your work. Do some research first before you send them your script. Make sure the company produces films a little like your story.

- Filmmaking students might need a good script to practice their skills on. Contact colleges and universities that run filmmaking courses.

Cell Phone Movie School

If you want to be taken seriously as a screenwriter, you need to make your script look as professional as you can. Make sure you present your work in the best way using correct spelling and grammar. That really makes a difference in how people think about your script when they read it. Ask someone else to check your script through for you. It's easy to miss mistakes that you typed yourself.

"I am a great believer that the material, if it's good enough, will make it to the top."

Cassian Elwes

Remember that people like to be flattered. If you tell a movie producer you love their films, you might get them on your side! They will have spent a lot of time and effort on their work and everyone loves praise!

ACTION!

The great day has arrived and a movie company has bought your script. This doesn't necessarily mean your job is over. Screenwriters sometimes work alongside a director.

Working with a Director

The director is the person who guides turning a screenplay into a movie. Some directors like to involve the screenwriter. The director is most likely to ask for changes during **preproduction**; that is, before the filming has started. Writers might be asked to rewrite parts of the script.

Cell Phone Movie School

It is very rare that a screenwriter would ever actually go **on set**. Once filming starts, usually control is handed over to the director. Any script changes would be done by either the director or writers hired by the director. The script often changes quite a bit from the original during this time.

Changing the Script During Filming

Your script will probably change during the filming process, too. The director and actors may make changes during their read-throughs. Once filming begins the script may still change. The original location may be too expensive to film in, or some scenes need to be cut due to timing. Once the film is shot, editors will make their changes, too.

Creating a Shooting Script

One change a director will certainly make is to turn your script into a **shooting script**. A shooting script gives technical information about how the movie is to be shot, such as camera angles, shot sizes, camera moves, and so on. The scenes are also numbered to help organize the production.

CU = Close up
MLS = Medium long
    shot (above the knees
    to above the head)
VLS = Very long shot

A script has spaces between the lines so the shooting instructions can be added in pencil.

FADE IN:

(1-1) EXT. A CABIN IN WOODS - DUSK
    VLS of cabin and woods
    A bear rustles through a trash can.

(1-2)   CU of trash can and bear
    TOM and RUTH appear walking through
    the trees. The bear runs off.

(1-3)   MLS of Tom and Ruth
                        TOM
        Did you hear that?

(1-4) CU of Tom

                        RUTH
            (startled)
        What was it?

(1-5)   CU of Ruth
    TOM shrugs his shoul.

GLOSSARY

abbreviations A shortened form of a written word or phrase used in place of the whole.

acts Main divisions of a play or a screenplay.

archetypes The original model from which something is copied.

audition A short performance to test the talents of a musician, singer, dancer, or actor.

close shot/close-up Film image taken at close range and showing the subject on a large scale.

collaborative Produced by or involving two or more parties working together.

cues A word, phrase, or action in a play serving as a signal for the next actor to speak or do something.

cut To remove from the script or movie.

dialogue Conversation given in a written story or play.

dissolve shot A gradual transition from one image to another.

establishing shot Usually the first shot of a new scene, to show where the action is taking place.

exterior Situated on the outside.

format The general organization or arrangement of something.

interior The internal or inner part of something; for example, the inside of a house.

misdirect A deception in which the attention of an audience is focused on one thing in order to distract its attention from another.

networking Interact with others to exchange information and develop professional or social contacts.

on set Taking place during or relating to the rehearsing of a play or film.

parentheticals Instructions inserted between parentheses.

plot The main story of a literary work or movie.

point A unit of measure used for measuring font size.

preproduction Work done on a movie or show, before full-scale production begins.

resolution The point in a story at which the chief dramatic complication is worked out.

scene A division of an act during which there is no change of set or break in time.

script The written text of a stage play, screenplay, or broadcast.

shooting script The version of a screenplay used during the production of a movie.

stage directions Instructions in the text of a screenplay indicating the movement, position, or tone of an actor, or the sound effects and lighting.

symbolism Using symbols to represent ideas or qualities.

transition The process or a period of changing from one state or condition to another.

typeface A particular design of type.

visualize Form a mental image of something.

voice-over A piece of narration in a film or broadcast, not accompanied by an image of the speaker.

wide shot Shows the entire object or human figure in some relation to its surroundings.

writer's block Being unable to think of what to write or how to proceed with writing.

FOR MORE INFORMATION

Books

Blofield, Robert. *How to Make a Movie in 10 Easy Lessons: Learn How to Write, Direct, and Edit Your Own Film Without a Hollywood Budget (Super Skills),* Lake Forest, CA: Walter Foster Jr., 2015.

Stowell, Louie *The Usborne Creative Writing Book,* London, UK: Usborne Publishing, 2016.

Websites

Due to the changing nature of Internet links, PowerKids Press has developed an online list of websites related to the subject of this book. This site is updated regularly. Please use this link to access the list:

www.powerkidslinks.com/mm/screenwriter

INDEX

abbreviations 20
actors 6, 22
acts 16, 17
adapting books 6
archetypes 12

Cabot, Meg 14
Celtx 10
characters 5, 6, 11, 12, 13, 14, 15, 16, 21, 24
close shot 19
close-up 23
courier 11
cues 11
cutting 17, 18, 19, 20, 25, 29

dialogue 4, 7, 15, 20, 21, 22, 23, 24
director 14, 17, 22, 23, 28
dissolve shots 18

editor 17, 18, 29
Elwes, Cassian 27
establishing shots 15

Fellowes, Julian 24
festivals 26
film students 26
format 10, 11

Hitchcock, Alfred 5

length 11
location 14, 15, 29

mannerisms 13
Mazin, Craig 19
McKee, Robert 8

misdirect 19
music 19

networking 4

obstacles 16

parentheticals 22, 23
plot 6, 9, 12, 16, 25
preproduction 28
producers 10, 27

resolution 16
rewrites 28, 29

scenes 15, 16, 17, 18, 19
script readers 10, 17
scriptwriting competitions 26
set designer 14, 23
setting 14, 15, 16, 17, 25
shooting scripts 29
special effects 7
stage directions 11, 22, 23
story ideas 6, 7, 8, 9
subtitles 15
symbolism 6

time 14, 15, 16, 18
title 25
title page 10
transitions 18, 19
typeface 11

voice-overs 21

wide shot 19
Wilder, Billy 17
writer's block 9